To mom, for everything.

Story Road

Copyright © 2021 BSC

i.

FOREWORD

Story Road, a new collection of prose and verse poems by Blaine Carrell, cuts right through the core of contemporary poetry: finding oneself through the deconstruction of family and romantic relationships. Carrell has a steady hand and a storyteller's charm, and what ties all this together are his acute observations of micro-gestures in real and imagined spaces.

Edinburgh, for instance, is the one in the middle of nowhere just south of Indianapolis. There's a big X where a major interstate crosses a major highway, but the area's claim to fame is a cluster of outlet malls, plural. One collection of "factories" (Cheesecake, Nike, The Gap, etc.) upside another set of shoppes full of seconds and rejects. Bargains galore.

This odd consumptive place is the backdrop for high drama, for who among us has not been dragged out shopping with Mom and ended up hiding in the racks ("Edinburgh: You")? Of course, for every call in these poems, there is a response ("Edinburgh: And Me"), in this case about how "she" dresses "him" funny and the hungry mouths he has to feed. The L/OVER section calls to the FAM/ILY section, and they both call out the SELF/ISH.

We find there are many selves, most of them solitary, all them charged with and by memory and working toward and against change:

Remotely remaining, I will remember

But something is in the way
Listening for where I am coming from

"Something in the Way"

There is no returning, to an idealized past or to anything or anyone that has departed in including yourself. That works in both the growing-up sense as well as in the heartbreak of letting go a once good thing. *Story Road* takes us on that journey, from origins to destinations and back to wandering, aimlessly, blissfully, wearily alone.

Tony Brewer
Author of 'Homunculus

TABLE OF CONTENTS

Foreword......*i*.
Prologue......*vi*.

FAM/ILY

The Farmer and the Tape Recorder 2
Renting de Mairan's Branch 4
Just Remember 5
As the Twigs Snap 6
Baking Soda 7
Last of the Dying (Glorious Day) 8
The Inspiration of Essence 9

L/OVER

A Billion Sparks 11
Glass Jar/Paper Cup 12
Edinburgh: You 13
Cincinnati 14
I Almost Got Her to Indianapolis 15
17 Geese 16
Politeness 17

SELF/ISH

The Gulled Man (3:30) 19
Someone Else's Mistake 20
Have One of Many 21
Roots and Mud 22
Edinburgh: And Me 23
When (My Hands) 24
Something in the Way 25
All in All 26

PROLOGUE

The writer is tired, but he is ready to exhaust everything that remains to his experience. He is keeping a searching eye open. His story is dormant but pulsing with the lifeblood of perception. His is a story of unfinished heroes. A story of people and places infinitely changing. The writer must be aware enough in order to ask the questions most important to him. His need is not to necessarily finish, but to both begin and finish with necessity.

One for yes

Two for no.

—Radiohead, "Bodysnatchers"

FAM/ILY

Story Road

2

The Farmer and the Tape Recorder

...

"Hellooo, Blaaaine Carrelll."

His digitized voice resonated throughout the halls of the funeral parlor with an unassuming authority even then. Family members thanked me, but I knew I was not the true focus of their gratitude. They were just so happy that he could be there on this side of things one more time.

"I didn't deserve a scholarship, but I sure could beat the gun."

In his youth he was fleet-footed. Maybe because deep down he knew there was nowhere for any of us to stay. Or maybe it was a way of ignoring anxiety. Part of me is glad that I was never his peer. But, then again, no one really was. He grew to admire his sadness, and so did I. That's why it was always easy for him to be a storyteller from the corner of a room.

"I just want them to be healthy and happy."

3

He grew up alongside his four daughters. He was never the picturesque model of a father, and it would be too simplistic to say that his compassion was strictly housed in duty. He was genuine, unkempt, and brash. He was overtly subtle, and an unwavering contortion of love and respect. He knew who he was, and that's all he could do. For me, the bones of the man will always be the color of a midday sun. But even the most vivid truths are protected in shades of gray.

"I'm not going to park my car next to my brother Charles. But that isn't the point, is it?"

4

Renting de Mairan's Branch

...

There was no mystery at fifteen. No ammunition required. Only a little bird flying somewhere in Africa waiting to become their adult version of familial responsibility. Or of something else just as fragrant. Like the day the wind pushed them off their comfortable branch. There was no mystery at fifteen, and for that little bird the world knew exactly what to do. Sit and wait. It had to ferment and foment so that it could fly back to me to tell me that mystery is anything but temporal. And I'm fine at forty-three to realize that sometimes our branches carry us, and sometimes we carry them.

Just Remember

...

A sisterly brotherhood
A mismatch in care
The tops of trees are for the birds,
Cardinals, and bears

When you left the cabbage patch
You broke my leaves
Our roots were at once
Severed — Left in tattered grieves

A conversation, of sorts,
Gets lost among our tall grass
And our feet get trampled
When we try walking our past

You were my first poem, B —
Kindling to my infant ember
Don't worry about all that now
Just remember.

As the Twigs Snap

...

As I sit on the edge of an autumn bonfire—no—I was never at the edge. I was always somewhere else inside those stars, maybe. I remember the cold air surrounding the tall fire. The scent of dead leaves, and the ash falling like nervous snowflakes. I remember how heavy my father's winter jacket felt around my boyish arms. I wasn't merely wearing it for protection against the ancient chill; I was becoming him. Or a sense of him. The part of me that, at that point, was the most true wasn't inside that denim uniform. It was uniting itself with who my father was. With who I knew he could be. The truest love between us never uttered a word. It sighed and shrugged as I looked up at the stars that belonged to only us.

Baking Soda

...

Sticks and stones always wasted my time
Could never fight for what I believed in
Only against those who didn't
Always front and center in my own emanation
Humor kills today just like it did then
Battles forthcoming will hold me close like a mother with her babe
Will vomit up the only words I know how to
This will be the living room sound system I reminisce with as Starlings gather around their glib feast
I hate time
The only picture I ever fell in love with.

Last of the Dying (Glorious Day)

...

It's thirty-four years and I'm still covering my eyes in a game of hide-and-go-seek Waiting for no one to be ready or not
Refusing to make amends for my future
A nine-year-old in perpetuity

The legs of this table I find myself hiding under are buckling
The legs of the one I'm hiding from are still stoic and young
I don't tell lies when I'm awake anymore
Only when I'm dreaming

I don't deny the fact that you're leaving
Only that I have a place to stay after you're gone.

The Inspiration of Essence

...

Only moments
Only words
Only a collection of visions that my senses have gathered
Only a single truth of what my experience has been

You were my first person
My arrival of individuality
My duality of detachment
My giving to the movement of change

You,
The fullness of embodiment,
The inspiration of essence,
The encompassment of the trail behind me

Not one sound
A song
Not one word
A story.

10

L/OVER

Story Road

A Billion Sparks

...

The names, the faces, the bodies, the voices, the simple moments of contortion. The hidden views, and the romanticized ruses. Was it James Byron Dean's fault? Charles Weedon Westover? Or was it my own artistic death wish? Why did I don the uniform of some anti-hero? Were the shootouts that important to the story? Were my high school fantasies that afraid of not being real? Whenever I would fall off the wagon, I would always find myself landing softly in someone else's makeshift bed. No white hat in sight. Just a billion sparks tired of the shakedowns.

Glass Jar/Paper Cup

...

He was an acquired boomerang. His curls were sexier than any kiss I've ever had. He was the first flashback of my clear-eyed innocence. We dangled our collective genealogies over cliffs of Camel Lights and CD players. We owed everything we ever did to the dead...and Véronique. Blame tastes just like resin when you can't remember a complete dream. That's late-night coffee and God's smile.

Edinburgh: You

...

Everything was an outlet for everything. The tears, the screams, the amnesia, and the sweater vests. You were a mother to everything that knew it couldn't die without failing. You were my mother. My piece of ass. My most faded love letter. I couldn't breathe without you because you knew exactly where I would be hiding. But I perfected the art of punishment; for both of us.
At least you can't take that away.
You can have everything else.

Cincinnati

...

Tangled in the wake of our wake
Love became a cognomen for exile
A fitting feast fed for one
Among the misery, laid bare, a vast and storied road
A simple song sung in soliloquy

I tarry in two directions
Stuck in a field of memory soldiers
I carry some in my heart
The others, on my back
I am, at once, before and after

Now; the signpost for discovery
The scar of existence
The hope for me.

I Almost Got Her to Indianapolis

...

Brighton Beach snapped a picture of someplace in my memory. On some edge of water, or long-lost ancestral happenstance.

C— entered my frame to tell me where she wanted to go. We studied each other instantaneously. It worked. The music of Louisana was playing way down low, but we still knew all the words.

Our hands worked together, off and on. Whetted. Strained. Softened. Grew. Hope about the future was never our concern. Now it's here.

We could never decide on the road, so we compromised on the bed.

16

17 Geese

...

Or nineteen. The number doesn't remember how you must have felt when I laid bare my extraordinary ability to be human. It doesn't keep in its bones the chill of that rainy afternoon, or morning. Satellites high in Earth's atmosphere will never remember the color of love between the notes of two singing bowls after they've transmitted a recording somewhere near Taos. You will never remember what I did after our last phone call. And I will never remember who called whom.

Politeness

...

Sunday is such a simple sting. Tomorrow, you remain this boy's atavistic three hundred sixty fifth regret.

Take a stand, J—; just not today.

What we must have tasted like before my panic attack. What we must taste like, still. Memory, do something with this face again.

Hide it inside the upside-down moonbeam. Or puzzle over it like a jigsaw. White blossom, break my lazy stride.

Sweet sadness, I found my comfort inside your constructive submission and nowhere else.

This is a song for you to dance naked to alone in your best life.

Is it enough?

SELF/ISH

Story Road

The Gulled Man (3:30)

...

The pain was born in feet
Stolen away by neighbors and churches
She had no idea how hot that fire was
She couldn't feel the sin
She wasn't supposed to
But he could
He always could
Even before he was a boy
And after he took it back
Well after.

Someone Else's Mistake

...

I never had to be determined. That wheel was set in motion long before I ever moved a muscle. It wasn't my fault that someone more earnest than myself found out my secret. I tried to keep it inside. I tried not to impose myself. "You're a miracle!" they would say. "Bless your heart." I resented them so much. I wasn't ever asked if I wanted to be responsible for their piousness. I was only ever the two-way mirror that permitted them to ignore their own shortcomings. I was someone else's mistake. And I didn't hate it. Not enough.

Have One of Many

...

I go by what I've been given. My piece of the puzzle. My star of the night. Now is what is. How long but a breath. When you can no longer see, you can give back to everything. When I sit in front of the night, alone and without knowing, I am amazed to be alive. In those moments I long not for a single sound except the crickets. They are what I was at nine years old. Alive and rememberless.

Roots and Mud

...

Someday a version of myself will be forever lying on the couch snoozing some Wednesday afternoon away while my better half is out there somewhere realizing gold isn't so precious of a metal after all. Remembering what it was like to unlock a gate without worrying about getting splinters. Sifting through cobwebs and ghosts and dead bats and discovering the life therein. This isn't a case of infinite regress. It's just a poem whose ending happened long before the pen touched the page.

Edinburgh: And Me

...

Her husband became an action potential
She dressed him in a suit of armor of lubrication and phone numbers
She sold his rights to a flock of the most restless birds she could find
He took his cue to leave from his ability to imagine marathons
She was his roundabout way to the nature of second chances
And his strongest push inside a parked car
He's a simple man sliding out of control away from her
But he always remembers to feed the birds.

When (My Hands)

...
My hands
Glass jars
Frightened bullets
Piercing the world
Past. New. Forgotten

These waves of Light keep stringing me along
When will I be done?
When will I say enough?

Something in the Way

...

All melancholies
Disconnected remembrances
A happy funeral

Cold and close place
Pensive spleen
Remotely remaining, I will remember

But something is in the way
Listening for where I am coming from
Adversely aged in winter
Insistent upon a planting Earth
Never wanting to be new
Entirely, inescapably enough

In time, this would wash over me as an art of war and poetry
A wisdom I would have to reason alone
A tempering of loss and gain
The most harmonious dissonance of my life.

All in All

...

He discovered he had no more room inside his mind for the vastness of everything.
Not one more purple flower could fragrant that dome.
Not one more child jumping rope could be found.
He was full from all the possibilities.
He was simply enough.
And that terrified him.

www.ingramcontent.com/pod-product-compliance
Lightning Source LLC
LaVergne TN
LVHW011901060526
838200LV00054B/4464